MW01316909

CREATIVE WAYS TO LOVE & ENCOURAGE HIM

ALYSSA BETHKE

Published in Kihei, HI, by Bethke Writings. Bethke Writings titles may be purchased in bulk for educational, business, fund-raising, or sales promotional use. For information, please e-mail info@bethkewritings.com.

The Library of Congress Cataloging-in-Publication
Data is on file with the Library of Congress
ISBN-13: 978-1-7342746-0-8

TABLE OF CONTENTS

HOW TO GET THE MOST OUT OF THIS BOOK.

First off, you rock. By getting these paired books and wanting to go through them with your significant other, you obviously are already dominating at life! We have prayed over this project and really believe it can be a fun way to cultivate a healthy relationship and bring back the joy and intimacy that sometimes gets lost amidst the every day activities.

To get the most out of this book, we'd first say lean in. Lean into the ideas, the spontaneity and the parts that stretch you the most. Don't be afraid to just go for it, have fun and create memories. We are firm believers that with these two books, whatever you put into it you will get out of it. Isn't that true with all our relationships as a whole? Also know that this is just a template. Some things won't fit for your relationship or you can't do based on certain locations, resources and other variables.

We have tried to make every day as applicable for everyone as possible. So with that being said, feel free to morph it, change it, adapt it and do whatever you need to do to get the most out of it. Because at the end of the day, the goal isn't to follow this book rigidly and "cross each day off your checklist" but rather it's to bring a fresh vibrancy and life back to your relationship.

Also, a quick note to the dating folks out there. Obviously we are married so we are coming from that perspective. We also wanted to write this so dating couples could have a useful tool! As mentioned above, you might have to morph it in a different way too. When not living together, some of these are a little harder since when you're dating you probably don't see each other every single day. So feel free to stretch this out over a few months or pick a couple per week.

JEFF & ALYSSA BETHKE

DAY ONE: PRAYER

Hands down the best thing you can do for your man is pray for him. I know a lot of times I'm tempted to do something else, something "better" or more noticeable. Which doing other things are great and totally part of pursuing him-hence this book! But prayer needs to be the foundation. I can't tell you how many times I've prayed for Jeff and then have been amazed at how God has moved in his heart. But even more so, I think prayer is what moves my heart to love and pursue him. I've found that when I'm consistently praying for Jeff, I'm way more patient, kind and gentle with him; I find myself cheering him on, being intentional and putting him above myself. A lot of times too, I don't know how to pursue Jeff. What could I do to show him I love him? That I'm thinking of him today? Lately, when I've asked the Lord to show me how to serve and love him, He leads me to do something for Jeff that ends up totally blessing Jeff that day. God knows our men the best, so why don't we ask Him to show us how to love them?

I will be the first to admit that I'm not consistent with praying for him, but I so long to grow in this area because when I do, it rocks! I think the lie that we can believe about prayer is that it's too easy, it won't do anything, we can do it better than God or we're just lazy. But the Lord loves it when we talk with Him. It doesn't need to be perfect, planned out or "spiritual." It just has to be real. You can talk to God about what you're hoping for your man, areas you'd love to see him grow in, questions you have or pray verses over him. I'll give you some verses today to get you started. Let's begin this journey with uplifting our men before our Father who is the One who knows and loves him the best.

Ephesians 6:10-20: Pray that he'd put on the armor of God today, being well suited for the spiritual battle that he faces each day.

Psalm 24:4: Pray that he'd be pure in heart, clinging to what is good and hating what is evil. Pray that he'd fight against any temptation to look or think on lustful thoughts.

Pray that he'd have wisdom as he goes about his day today, making decisions.

JOURNAL BELOW:

WRITE WHAT YOU LEARNED TODAY, HOW IT WENT AND WHAT MEMORIES WERE MADE.

DAY TWO: SCRIP- TURE

Scripture is full of prayers and songs of praises! Throughout the Old Testament we see men and women talking to God and giving Him praise for all that He's done. Then, in the New Testament, we read letters written by the apostles that have prayers written out that they're praying for believers in certain towns and cities. Many times, those same prayers have been my prayers for my family, friends and myself. I love praying through certain verses, because as I do so, it draws me closer to knowing who the Lord is as well as gives me wisdom in how to pray for those I love. Because truth be told, sometimes I just don't know what to pray for.

Going along with yesterdays call to action, today I'd like you to choose a verse to memorize and pray over your man for this next month. Maybe it's a verse you've been reading about lately, or something that the Lord lays on your heart. Write it out and frame it. Give it to your man, telling him you're praying this verse over him this month. Even if he doesn't know how to respond to this gesture, or doesn't say much, I know it'll really touch his heart knowing you're praying for him.

JOURNAL BELOW:

WRITE WHAT YOU LEARNED TODAY, HOW IT WENT AND WHAT MEMORIES WERE MADE.

DAY THREE: SERVICE

Galatians 5:13b, "...serve one another in love."

Jeff's all time favorite thing is getting his feet massaged. If there is one way I can serve him, it's that. If we're debating over something and we decide to bet on it, if I throw out that I'll massage his feet if I lose, he's all in! If I don't know what to get him for Christmas, I always have lotion and a foot massage to lean back on. It's just the best in his book. And if I'm totally honest with you, I have to talk myself in to doing it every time because GROSS. I mean, I adore my husband, but touching feet isn't on my list of favorite things to do. However, when I see how much Jeff loves it, it gives me joy. I love being able to serve him in this way; in a way that I know really blesses him. It helps him relax and shows him that I'm thinking of him.

Today, give your man a foot massage (or back if he likes that better). It doesn't have to be a 60-minute massage from the Four Seasons! Even just 5 minutes shows them that you are thankful for him and his hard work.

JOURNAL BELOW:

WRITE WHAT YOU LEARNED TODAY, HOW IT WENT AND WHAT MEMORIES WERE MADE.

DAY FOUR: SNACK TIME

The other day Jeff was taking a nap but I knew he'd be getting up soon and he'd need a little snack because dinner was still a ways off. I looked in our fridge and there were celery sticks already cut up. So I decided to just throw together some ants on a log (celery with peanut butter and raisins). OK, I didn't "just throw them together." They're actually a little more time consuming than I realized! Thanks, mom, for all those hours you spent making me them growing up! When Jeff woke up, he was a little cranky. I'm just being real with ya'll here. I mean, let's be honest, sometimes you wake up from a nap feeling like you just won the lottery. And other times you feel worse than when you fell asleep. This was the latter for my man that day. But then when he saw the ants on a log on the kitchen counter waiting for him, his whole face lit up and his entire demeanor changed. He ate those bad boys, and was a whole new man.

Today, make or put together your man's favorite snack. If your man loves pistachios, just buy a bag for him at the store, he will love it! Or it can be super simple like cut up apple slices or microwavable popcorn. Just think of something that he likes and have it ready for him when he gets home or when you see him today.

JOURNAL BELOW:

WRITE WHAT YOU LEARNED TODAY, HOW IT WENT AND WHAT MEMORIES WERE MADE.

DAY FIVE: DINNER TIME

Whoever said, “Food is the way to a man’s heart,” hit it right on the head! No truer words have been said when it comes to my husband. He loves eating and he loves food, good food. (I mean, who am I kidding? SO DO I!) If you ever come to our house for dinner and we are eating something that Jeff loves, he’ll give me a standing ovation and bang his hands on the table (sure makes a girl feel good). Kinsley, our 2 year old daughter, does the same thing now when she likes something. It’s too cute!

I’m guessing that for the majority of us, your man likes food too. And even if he isn’t a foodie, I know he appreciates a good meal that is provided for him. This week, plan to make him a dinner that he really enjoys. For some of you, this totally excites you! You love to cook. You’re pulling out your Pioneer Woman recipe books, scrolling through Pinterest to find the perfect meal. Others of you are probably wanting to ignore this whole mention of making dinner and skip ahead because cooking is just not something you do or enjoy. So I’m just gonna say this-grace and freedom on you!! If you love to cook, then you go girl! You get at it! But if it’s not your thing, that’s OK. You don’t have to be Martha Stewart in the kitchen. Either make something really simple or go grab take out from one of his favorite restaurants. There’s nothing to prove to him or yourself. It’s just showing him you care by providing a good meal. (And if that good meal is a happy meal from McDonald’s because that’s what he likes, then awesome!)

JOURNAL BELOW:

WRITE WHAT YOU LEARNED TODAY, HOW IT WENT AND WHAT MEMORIES WERE MADE.

DAY SIX: PRAY FOR YOUR MAN

I'm longing to grow in praying for Jeff more consistently. When he's traveling, I find myself praying for him much more often, probably because we don't talk nearly as much. So I take my concerns and his heart to the Lord instead of just relying on myself to love him. But when we're home together, I often forget to pray for him because I'm talking to him all the time and I think I just take him, or rather the fact that I'm with him all the time, for granted. It's easy for me to pray for everything else, like my kids, my worries or friends, over him. Why is that? But on top of just longing to pray for him more, I also want to grow in praying over him; when he's right there besides me, to put my hand on him and lift him up to the Father. Sometimes when Jeff's struggling with something, he'll come to me and ask me to pray for him. And every time, it's like I'm caught off guard. Like I forget that that's something God calls us to do. And every time I do it, it's so beautiful. Jeff is totally vulnerable with me, humble to ask for help, and I get to join with him, going to the Father with his concerns. What an honor!

On top of all that, whenever I'm having a hard day or just flat out so emotional, Jeff will always ask if he can pray for me. And it's one of the absolute sweetest things. I think it's the way I feel most loved from him. Because truth be told, sometimes I'm just way too weak to even ask Jesus for help (or maybe too prideful). And then Jeff steps in for me and asks on my behalf.

You get to have the same honor of praying for your man, while he's right there with you. It may feel awkward at first or you may be embarrassed or shy. But don't be! It is a huge privilege and one that will not only bless your man but also bring you two together as you go before the Father together.

Today, ask him if you can pray over him. It could be before he goes to work, before bed tonight or just in the middle of the day. Thank the Lord for this man of yours and pray for his heart and mind; for his work, protection and purity.

JOURNAL BELOW:

WRITE WHAT YOU LEARNED TODAY, HOW IT WENT AND WHAT MEMORIES WERE MADE.

DAY SEVEN: ENTER HIS WORLD

Part of loving someone is doing what they love to do; *entering their world*. For instance, one way I show Kinsley that I love her is by intentionally playing with her. To do that, I need to enter her world and do what she loves to do. So, you may find me on all fours, crawling around our coffee table chasing her. Or, I may put on her princess crown and sit criss cross on the floor with all her stuffed animals surrounding us as I read a book to her. I don't do this all the time and I really do have to consciously think how I can be intentional with her somedays. But when I do it, not only does she love it, but I love it because I get to be a kid again and just love being with my little girl.

Guys are the same! One way that they bond with someone is by doing a shared activity. Jeff can go hiking, paddle boarding or shoot some hoops with another guy and automatically they're connected in some way. In relationships, I think it can be easy (especially in marriage) to forget this and to get into the habit of talking and then doing your own things. Right now Jeff and I are in the newborn stage with a toddler, we're exhausted a lot. We give all we have when our kids are awake, but by the time they go to sleep, we're so tired, we just go to bed ourselves. Or we sit on the couch doing our own things like reading or scrolling through Instagram and Facebook. And some nights, that's totally OK! But if we go a few nights in a row like that, we start to feel disconnected. So, we're trying to be more intentional with each other and one way for us to do that is for me to enter his world. What does Jeff like to do? And how can I hop in and do it with him?

Think of one thing that your man loves to do. It may be a sport, a certain genre of movie, a book that he's currently reading, working out, cooking, gardening, music, cars, etc. Today (or sometime this week) do that hobby *with* him. Go see that movie he's been dying to see with him in the theatre, go watch his softball game and cheer him on, pick up a copy of the book he's reading and read it together, listen to him play guitar, ask him to show you something about cars. Enter HIS world this week.

JOURNAL BELOW:

WRITE WHAT YOU LEARNED TODAY, HOW IT WENT AND WHAT MEMORIES WERE MADE.

DAY EIGHT: BREAKFAST IS THE MOST IMPORTANT MEAL OF THE DAY

About 6 months into dating Jeff, he got a new job and had to travel a lot. I MEAN A LOT. Like every week. Some trips he would land in Seattle at 2pm and have to fly back out at 5pm that same night. To say it was hard for me is an understatement! I mean, I loved that he was loving what he was doing and was so filled up but man, I missed my guy.

For one of his trips, I got to drive him to the airport early that morning because I didn't have work that day. I hadn't seen him much, so we decided we'd stop at the nearest Starbucks by the airport for a quick coffee date before he flew out. Obviously Starbucks has coffee (mmmm coffee) and pastries but I wanted to make it a special little coffee break for us, so I whipped up some cream cheese peach muffins for Jeff. 1. Because he loves cream cheese 2. Because he loves anything peach. 3. Because I straight up love muffins. I put them in a basket with napkins and a note and brought them into Starbucks with us.

Looking back now that I'm married and know my husband, that was just a little appetizer for him, maybe even an appetizer to the appetizer! A muffin is just a snack to Jeff; he needs the full meal deal. Eggs, potatoes, toast. Regardless, he loved those muffins, but I think even more so, he loved that I *thought of him* and made something that had his favorites in it. And really, it didn't take that much of an effort on my part.

Today, think of a fun breakfast treat that your man would enjoy (muffins, cinnamon rolls, donuts, bagels, etc.). Meet up with him tomorrow morning and share your treat together. If that's not possible because he leaves so early, then leave it where he'll find it in the morning (or take it to his work) with a cute little note just saying you were thinking of him and you hope he has a great day.

JOURNAL BELOW:

WRITE WHAT YOU LEARNED TODAY, HOW IT WENT AND WHAT MEMORIES WERE MADE.

DAY NINE: EYE CONTACT

Words are powerful. They can either build up or tear down. Words can either destroy a relationship or make it flourish. Jeff is so good about telling me every day that he loves me and is thankful for me. He constantly is telling me that I'm beautiful and a wonderful wife and mom. Can I be honest with you? Most of the time, especially lately, I sure don't *feel* beautiful. I probably already botched up being a wonderful wife and mom that day by a comment I made or by being impatient or selfish. But when Jeff looks me in the eyes and speaks those words over me, I start to believe them instead of getting bogged down by the lies I can so easily believe about myself. And that gives me life. It gives me hope. It helps me to see myself the way God sees me and it helps me to be a better wife and mom. Insecurities fly out the door. Feelings of being overwhelmed or anxious are exchanged for courage to do the task God's given me.

It can be easy to not speak life into our men because we're too busy but man, is it important! So today, look your man in the eyes and tell him how thankful you are for him and at least one thing that you love about him. Think of something specific like, "I love how you provide for our family" or "I love how you listen to people and make them feel heard."

JOURNAL BELOW:

WRITE WHAT YOU LEARNED TODAY, HOW IT WENT AND WHAT MEMORIES WERE MADE.

DAY TEN: 10 THINGS

A few weeks ago I was praying for Jeff and had asked the Lord to show me how I could encourage him that day. It had been a week after I had given birth to our son Kannon, so I felt pretty tapped out and not able to do much for Jeff. I was getting ready in our bathroom and saw our dry eraser marker in a basket. You know, you never know when you need to write a little note on your bathroom mirror! So I grabbed that bad boy and wrote out 10 things I loved about Jeff on his side of the mirror. It took me probably 5 minutes. It wasn't pretty or designed or super thought out. It was just a little overflow of my heart letting him know that I love him, see him and am thankful for all he does. Later that day, I was sitting on our couch, when he came out and told me how much that list meant to him. It totally made his day! It was just a small gesture that made all the difference that day.

Today, write out 10 things that you love and appreciate about your man. Write it on his bathroom mirror, in a note or text.

JOURNAL BELOW:

WRITE WHAT YOU LEARNED TODAY, HOW IT WENT AND WHAT MEMORIES WERE MADE.

DAY ELEVEN: HOW HE'S GROWN

Life can be discouraging at times and we can get bogged down by thinking of all the things we aren't doing right, what we need to do differently, what we need to change or how we failed in a particular task or moment. I think too, often it's harder to see what God is doing in us or the ways we've grown. But God is always at work in our lives and we are always growing if we're seeking Him. There is always fruit, even if it's just a seed.

When you're doing life with someone, it's so important to point out areas you see them growing in because often they don't see it themselves. There is nothing like hearing someone, especially someone close to you, tell you you're doing an awesome job in this area or how you've become more patient, gentle or kind in this way. It's so encouraging and gives you hope that you are growing, even though you're not perfect and still have room to change.

Today, tell your man at least one area that you've seen him grow in lately and how proud you are of him. If you're not sure what that is, spend some time praying and thinking of the past couple of weeks. When you spend time praying for your man, you're more attuned to what God is doing in his life. *Note: When you tell him how he's grown today, don't tell him how bad he was before at something! Just mention how you've seen him be a certain way lately and how proud you are of him. For instance, "Babe, I've seen you be really patient with your clients this week and I'm so proud of you." Or "Thank you for taking out the trash this week without me even having to ask you. I so appreciate that. Thank you for being on it, and serving me in that way."

JOURNAL BELOW:

WRITE WHAT YOU LEARNED TODAY, HOW IT WENT AND WHAT MEMORIES WERE MADE.

DAY TWELVE: RESPON- SIBILI- TIES

I remember when Jeff and I first got married, we argued over making the bed for like the first two years! I love a made bed. It's my jam. When I'm getting things done, it's the first thing I do. I feel frazzled if it's unmade and I hate looking into our room if the bed is all messy. I'm totally OK leaving it unmade if we're running late somewhere, but otherwise, I like it nice and neat. Jeff on the other hand, thought it was a waste of time because we're just going to sleep in it that night and get it messy again. Can anyone else relate to this debate? We went back and forth forever. Then finally one day, Jeff got me. I wouldn't say he felt the same way about needing it to be made to get other things done or to feel organized but he realized that regardless of his opinion, the fact was that making the bed was important to me and it really served me to have it made. One day I walked in,and it was made. And I'll add that he did a better job at making it than I did!

For the most part, I still end up making the bed most of the time. But on those days that I walk into our room after breakfast and he's made the bed, I always stop and look and feel so loved in that moment. It's a small gesture, but I know that Jeff was thinking of me and did it for me. He knew that it would help and serve me to do it. And although it's his bed too, I know he did it for me because he doesn't really care about a made bed.

Today, think of a responsibility that he has and do it for him. It doesn't have to be something that you guys think differently about! Think of a task that he always does that you could do for him. It could be taking out the trash, washing his car, making his lunch for the next day, bringing snacks to his meeting so he doesn't have to, etc.

JOURNAL BELOW:

WRITE WHAT YOU LEARNED TODAY, HOW IT WENT AND WHAT MEMORIES WERE MADE.

DAY THIRTEEN: CAR SUR-PRISES

Last week we celebrated Mother's Day. I had really been wanting eyelash extensions FOREVER, so I finally got them. Because who has time to put on make up with a toddler and newborn!? I told Jeff that was my Mother's Day gift. All that to say, I wasn't expecting anything on Mother's Day, I just wanted to be with my family and celebrate my mom. After we had a special breakfast and played in the yard, both the kids fell asleep (oh how I cherish you sweet nap time), so I told Jeff I was going to take a bath and lay down for a bit. While I was rocking Kins asleep in her room, Jeff went ahead and got my bath ready. He filled it with bath salts and bubble bath, lit a candle, put on music, grabbed my book and wrote a little note that said "I LOVE YOU." When I came out of Kinsley's room, I smelled the bath salts and went into the bathroom amazed. Talk about an amazing husband! How thoughtful was he!? You know the funny thing though? Amidst all that wonderfulness, my favorite part was the little note that said "I LOVE YOU." I know I'm a words person. I feel the most loved by written word. And I'll take it in any form-texts, emails, cards. But there was something just so sweet about seeing Jeff's handwriting on that bright blue card in bold font. I still have it hanging up in my bathroom mirror.

Little surprises that say "Hey, I'm thinking of you," are always sweet and special. It's such a good feeling to know that someone has you on his or her mind. And it can be the littlest thing! Today, put a little something in his car as a sweet surprise. It could be a little note that says "I LOVE YOU," your picture on his dashboard or his favorite candy bar. Anything that says you're thinking of him.

JOURNAL BELOW:

WRITE WHAT YOU LEARNED TODAY, HOW IT WENT AND WHAT MEMORIES WERE MADE.

DAY FOURTEEN: MAKE IT KNOWN

If you're on Facebook or Instagram, I'm sure you've seen ladies post about their men and use #MCM (Man Crush Monday). Although I always forget to post about Jeff on Mondays just like I always forget to do a #TBT (Throw Back Thursday) until Friday-I love this concept! I think it's so great to tell others how thankful we are for our men, especially in a culture where women put down their men in front of others. Let's be women who speak kindly about our men, who honor them, respect them and cheer them on.

Today, post a Facebook or Instagram post about how thankful you are for your man. Use #31creativeways so we can all see it and cheer each other on as women who honor their men!

JOURNAL BELOW:

WRITE WHAT YOU LEARNED TODAY, HOW IT WENT AND WHAT MEMORIES WERE MADE.

DAY FIFTEEN: OUR STORY

One of my favorite questions to ask a couple is how they met or when did they know that was the person they wanted to spend the rest of their lives with. The best is hearing the couple go back and forth, playing off of each other and hearing them recount their story. As they talk, you can still see the sparkle in their eye and by the end of the story, its like they are closer in some way. They are enjoying one another more than when they sat down because they're reminded of how sweet their story is and how much they love each other.

Bring a little sparkle back today by writing a note to your guy telling him your meeting story and when you started to fall for him. It can be a long letter or just a simple note to remind him of your beginnings.

JOURNAL BELOW:

WRITE WHAT YOU LEARNED TODAY, HOW IT WENT AND WHAT MEMORIES WERE MADE.

DAY SIXTEEN: DREAMS

Jeff and I do this journal together where we ask each other the same 6 specific questions every week (well, we're trying to do it every week). It's a game changer. Truly. Talking about these questions each week helps us to get on the same page and breeds a lot more grace and support in our marriage. It gives us a vision for the week and a short-term vision for our relationship.

One of the questions we ask each other is, "What dreams or thoughts have been on your mind this week?" Now, my husband and I are both dreamers, so this question isn't too difficult for us. However, Jeff is an extreme visionary, so every week he has a *new* dream to share! Which at times can be hard for this anxious little heart of mine. Always something new. Always something changing. Always something in the works. The more I'm married to Jeff though, I'm realizing how important it is to really listen to him dreams and to encourage him in them. Even if it sounds crazy or totally 100% out of my comfort zone. I can share my questions, of course, but I need to cheer him on in it and dream with him first. When I do that, it's like he's a new man, fearless and able to conquer anything. But when I let my anxious heart get in the way and give him looks like, "Oh boy, another dream..." it completely crushes him.

I realize that Jeff is an extreme case of a dreamer and most likely your man doesn't always have a new thing on the horizon. However, all of us have dreams and all have us have thoughts throughout the week of something we're hoping to do, to accomplish, to change. For instance, in this season of my life right now, I don't have a whole lot of dreams that I'm thinking of. However, I want to have a certain couple over for dinner next week, I want to take Kinsley to the strawberry farm next weekend and I really want to join a barre class to tone up a bit. Thoughts. Dreams.

Today, ask your man a thought or dream that he's been chewing on this week. Something he can't stop thinking of or something that keeps coming back to his mind. Listen as he shares and dream with him. Encourage him in a certain endeavor or pray over it for him.

JOURNAL BELOW:

WRITE WHAT YOU LEARNED TODAY, HOW IT WENT AND WHAT MEMORIES WERE MADE.

DAY SEVEN-TEEN: CANDY CRUSH

When Jeff and I first started dating, it was long distance. He was in Oregon going to college and I was across the Pacific Ocean in Hawaii doing an internship at a church. Although long distance definitely has it pits-like you're not together! But one good thing is it forces you to be creative. Like really creative. I mean, when you can't hang out, go on dates or see each other at church, you're forced to find ways to show each other that you care other than the phone.

One Valentine's Day I decided to make Jeff a candy gram. I went to the store and bought as many different candy bars that I could find. Then I put a bunch of construction paper together like a book and wrote him a love letter using the candy bars as fill in words. Next thing I know, I'm getting a telephone call with Jeff on the other end, munching on a candy bar, proclaiming how awesome my candy gram was! HE LOVED IT.

Now, even if your man is super healthy or doesn't really do candy, I guarantee he'll love the candy gram because it's thoughtful and creative. So, go to the grocery store or gas station and pick up some candy bars to make your own candy gram for your man. Some good ones to get are *Symphony, 1,000 grand, Milky Way, Hot Tamales, & Big Hunk.* Make your message as short or as long as you like. You don't have to be a poet to do it! Just be creative and have fun.

JOURNAL BELOW:

WRITE WHAT YOU LEARNED TODAY, HOW IT WENT AND WHAT MEMORIES WERE MADE.

DAY EIGHT–TEEN: LET'S GO ON A DATE

To this day, Jeff will still tell you that one of his all time favorite dates that I took him on was when he came out to Maui to visit me. My youth pastor had let me borrow his truck for the night, so I couldn't wait to take Jeff out somewhere. However, being an intern, I had no money. Like zilch. So I packed a special picnic dinner for us. You know, PB & J's, apples and cookies. I filled up two Nalgene bottles with water and added some crystal light peach packets in them because I knew how much Jeff loved peach flavoring. We drove down the street awhile and then parked where we could back up to the beach. We climbed in the back of the truck, put a blanket down and ate our picnic dinner as we watched the sun sink into the ocean. We talked, laughed and had the best time!

Plan a special date with your guy this week. It doesn't have to be elaborate or expensive, just something that is intentional and brings you two together. Think of something that *he* would love to do. If you need to get a babysitter, do it, or you can always do something when the kids go to bed. It doesn't even have to be that long. If you only can fit in an hour, that's perfect. You'll be surprised at how much you can pack into an hour when you're both being intentional with each other. Some ideas are: have a bonfire, play a board game, chat over a fruit and cheese platter.

JOURNAL BELOW:

WRITE WHAT YOU LEARNED TODAY, HOW IT WENT AND WHAT MEMORIES WERE MADE.

JOURNAL BELOW:

WRITE WHAT YOU LEARNED TODAY, HOW IT WENT AND WHAT MEMORIES WERE MADE.

DAY NINE-TEEN: SPECIAL PLACE

We all have our favorite places to go and hang out. They become "our places." Maybe you have a favorite coffee shop you like to hang out at, a store that you always go to or a park that you love to go and read at. For me, there's this walk down the road a bit that is right on the ocean. It's gorgeous, truly breathe taking. It's about 1.5 miles long and lines up with all the resorts on the water. It curves and has hills and is lined with tropical greenery. As you walk you can see all the boats and ships that go sailing by. Some days you can spot whales out in the ocean deep or turtles swimming by the shore. It's my all time favorite place in the whole world. I've spent countless hours walking that path praying, dreaming, processing and having heart to hearts with friends.

Jeff has never been someone to go for walks. He likes working out but not if it feels like working out! Give him basketball, paddle boarding or swimming, anything that's fun and action packed. But recently he's been up for walking with me. I used to have to beg him to come with me but now if I mention I'm going on a walk, half the time he jumps at the chance to go with me! And I can't tell you how much it means to me. I love having that intentional time with him and I love the fact that he's wanting to join me on something I love doing. So, when he goes with me on my favorite walk, it's like he's shouting from the rooftops, "I LOVE YOU ALYSSA!"

Think of one of your man's favorite spots to hang out and go with him to that spot this week. If it's Crossfit or his gym, go watch him or buy a one-day pass to work out together. If it's a music store, go look at instruments together. If it's a food truck, go get lunch together. Whatever is his spot, go there together this week.

JOURNAL BELOW:

WRITE WHAT YOU LEARNED TODAY, HOW IT WENT AND WHAT MEMORIES WERE MADE.

DAY TWENTY: OH, HEY HAND-SOME

Laughing is one of my favorite things to do. Tell me a good joke and it'll make my whole day. When I was in junior high, my friend and I use to send each other pick-up lines from this one website. We got the biggest kick out of the ones people came up with and bonus! The website had a new pick up line every day. I always wanted a guy to use one of the pick up lines on me. I mean, how could a girl say no to, "Looks like you dropped something- my jaw!"

Today, find a good pick-up line and use it on your guy. Text it, email it, write it in a note. Maybe even have a different one for him every hour! Whatever you do, show him you like him while giving him a good laugh.

JOURNAL BELOW:

WRITE WHAT YOU LEARNED TODAY, HOW IT WENT AND WHAT MEMORIES WERE MADE.

DAY TWENTY-ONE: MOVIE NIGHT

Jeff and I love our movie nights. We don't get to the movie theatre much these days but one of our favorite things to do is pick a good movie on Netflix or Amazon and cuddle up on the couch together. Jeff makes this crazy good popcorn that we put in our special white popcorn bowls and Aslan, our dog, sits by my feet drooling the whole time I chomp away.

As I am writing this, I'm realizing that for the most part, we always watch a movie that I want to watch. Now, don't get me wrong. Jeff will agree to the movie and want to watch it too but it's never one on the top of his list. He always goes ahead with one that I really want to see because he's so sweet and because I'm a lot more picky movie watcher. I mean, I just really love my Rom Coms (romantic comedies)! This week, watch a movie with your man but let him choose the movie. Pop some popcorn, get some candy and cuddle up together.

JOURNAL BELOW:

WRITE WHAT YOU LEARNED TODAY, HOW IT WENT AND WHAT MEMORIES WERE MADE.

DAY TWENTY-TWO: ART OF THANK YOU

One thing that makes for a successful relationship is found in two words- "THANK YOU." Showing that you notice what he's doing and are grateful is monumental in a relationship. It shows that you see him and you appreciate him. Sometimes it can be easy to get caught up in all the things that he's not doing or ways you wish he would change. But that can be toxic.

When Jeff says thank you to me for doing the things that I normally do everyday, it makes me want to keep serving him and gives me joy in the midst of it. Sometimes he'll stop me from what I'm doing, look me in the eye and thank me for something specific. It makes me break out in the biggest smile; it's the best.

This week, focus on saying thank you for the big and little things that your man does. For taking out the trash, clearing your plate, opening your door, making you coffee, etc. Today specifically, think of one thing he's done for you, look him in the eye and say thank you.

JOURNAL BELOW:

WRITE WHAT YOU LEARNED TODAY, HOW IT WENT AND WHAT MEMORIES WERE MADE.

DAY TWENTY-THREE: DRAW A PICTURE

Last weekend we celebrated Kinsley's 2nd birthday. Since Kinsley's favorite thing in the whole world is swimming, we bought her a blow up pool complete with a slide and ball activities. We had a little pool party with a few of her closest friends. She had a blast! Literally it was the best day of her life. She giggled and smiled the whole morning. Her friends all brought her a little gift and all of them included a homemade card. Her friend Ace drew her a stick picture of the two of them together and handed it to her as soon as he saw her. She looked at it, pointed to each stick figure and got the biggest smile on her face.

Cards can sometimes be the best gift of all. I love how little kids draw pictures for people. I have a handful hanging up on my refrigerator right now, displayed as the pieces of artwork that they are.

This may sound silly, but draw a picture for your man today. If you're an incredible artist, then draw something amazing! But if you're like me and stick figures is about as good as it gets, that's OK too! Really, this days action is all about bringing the childlike wonder back into a relationship. It's just something fun and thoughtful. Draw it on a sticky note or construction paper. Draw a picture of your man and point out characteristics that he has that you love. Or draw a picture of the two of you together. Maybe draw a picture of when you met, your favorite date or one of your favorite memories. Or draw a picture of something you'd like to do together one day. Whatever it is, I'm sure he'll cherish it as Kinsley cherished her homemade birthday cards.

JOURNAL BELOW:

WRITE WHAT YOU LEARNED TODAY, HOW IT WENT AND WHAT MEMORIES WERE MADE.

DAY TWENTY-FOUR: CHEER-LEADER

I hosted a mom's gathering this last spring with a handful of women who I really wanted to get know more. Each week they'd come over for a time of fellowship and learning. An older mom would come and share each week about what they have learned as a mom or wife or what God's taught them over the years. Not only did our group become tight-knit, we also got to be encouraged by these older women and shaped by their wisdom. One of the ladies who came to teach shared about loving and enjoying her husband. She told us that we as wives are called to be our husbands' biggest cheerleaders. We are to stand by their side, support them, listen well, pray diligently and encourage them. I had known to support and encourage Jeff but I had never heard it quite phrased that way before-be their biggest cheerleader. I love it that it gives me an awesome picture in my head of one of the main roles as a wife. Even if you're just dating, being a cheerleader for your man is important! Our guys need to know we believe in them and are for them.

Take a picture of yourself today, holding up a sign that says "GO __(fill in your man's name)____!" Send it to him sometime today, letting him know that you are cheering him on!

JOURNAL BELOW:

WRITE WHAT YOU LEARNED TODAY, HOW IT WENT AND WHAT MEMORIES WERE MADE.

DAY TWENTY-FIVE: BUCKET LIST

We have these friends who pretty much rock at life. They're some of my favorite people ever and a couple that I really look up to. Last year their church focused on loving and pursuing your spouse and encouraged their congregation to go on date with each other every week. They called it 52 in 15 (2015). As in, 52 dates in 52 weeks. At the end of the year, the couples that actually did 52 dates were entered into a contest to win a vacation cruise for a week. It's an awesome concept if you ask me! The whole purpose behind it is to encourage married couples to invest in their marriage. Well, this year, our friends are doing it again, but for their dates they made a bucket list; a list of 52 dates that they want to do with one another. It's been so fun to follow them on Instagram and see the fun dates they do. Some have been making a fruit pizza together, going on a picnic, and making a playlist that reflects their spouse.

Sit down with your guy today or sometime this week and make a bucket list of dates that you want to do together. You don't need to do 52! But get at least 10 down that the two of you can do together. Make the bucket list making a little date in itself! Get some yummy snacks, a good drink and have fun scheming together.

JOURNAL BELOW:

WRITE WHAT YOU LEARNED TODAY, HOW IT WENT AND WHAT MEMORIES WERE MADE.

DAY TWENTY-SIX: COMPLIMENTS

"Pleasant words are a honeycomb, sweet to the soul and healing to the bones." Proverbs 16:24

Have you ever had someone give you a card or send you a random text that tells you how special you are and even has a little list of character traits you possess that they love and admire? It's the absolute best. And if you're like me, it usually comes at just the right moment that you need it.

My parents and friends would give me little notes growing up with these sweet sayings but the one I remember most was an unexpected card from one of my close friends and mentors when I was interning at the church. It had been a long, hard day and to be honest, I was in a season of a lot of growth. Which is a nice way of saying I was a hot mess! The Lord was stretching me and growing me in ways I'd never knew were possible. I walked into our office and there on my computer was an envelope with my name beautifully written on the top of it. I opened it up and there was a list of things she saw in me that were beautiful. Tears stung in my eyes because amidst all my mess, there was a deep beauty that God was creating and continuing to perfect in me.

Words can make all the difference in someone's day. Send a little text to your man today with at least 5 genuine things that you love about him.

JOURNAL BELOW:

WRITE WHAT YOU LEARNED TODAY, HOW IT WENT AND WHAT MEMORIES WERE MADE.

DAY TWENTY-SEVEN: JUST ASK

This past year, Jeff has started to ask me before the day starts or after a heart to heart, what he can do to help me that day? How can he serve me today? And each time that he asks me, my heart softens and calms. Sometimes, I actually do have some things for him to do that would really be helpful to me. But for the most part, it brings me peace and encouragement that he just asks. It shows me that he's thinking of me and reminds me that we're a team. I'm not alone. I don't have to do everything on my own but he's there to help me in any way. Which, for me, is so encouraging because I tend to get overwhelmed easily.

Ask your guy if there's anything you can do to help him today. Is there any way you can serve him? Be prepared if he does have something for you to do and do it cheerfully! But know that just the asking will encourage him too.

JOURNAL BELOW:

WRITE WHAT YOU LEARNED TODAY, HOW IT WENT AND WHAT MEMORIES WERE MADE.

DAY TWENTY-EIGHT: ABC

"ABC
It's easy as 1,2,3
As simple as do, re, mi
ABC 1,2,3
Baby, you and me girl."

Today's task will take a little more time and thought but I promise you it will be something that will really bless and honor him.

Pinterest is full of cute little ways to show your man you love him. One year for Valentine's Day I rummaged through a whole list of DIY ideas of things I could make for Jeff. I saw this deck of cards that they punched a hole through on top and put together. On each card, they had written a characteristic trait that they loved about their man. It was so cute! And so I went ahead and whipped (well, not quite!) one up for Jeff. I remember seeing the look on his face when he opened it and read each one. He was so touched that I had spent so much time coming up with 52 things that I love about him. It's still in his side table by his bed as a little reminder that I love him so.

For today's task, I won't ask you to come up with 52 things you love about your man (feel free too though)! However, 26 things seems pretty doable. Get 26 little cards together, 26 sticky notes or just a sheet of paper and write out the ABC's. Come up with a character trait or something that your man does that you love for each letter of the alphabet. It doesn't have to be poetic at all or even artsy. Just dot down 26 things you love about him.

JOURNAL BELOW:

WRITE WHAT YOU LEARNED TODAY, HOW IT WENT AND WHAT MEMORIES WERE MADE.

DAY TWENTY-NINE: DRINK IT UP

When Jeff and I first started dating, I thought one of the ways a guy shows you he loves you and is pursuing you is by bringing you your favorite drink from time to time. In all fairness I did grow up in Seattle, home of the coffee bean. (OK, it's totally not the home of the coffee bean, but man do we love our coffee there!). So I frequented coffee shops. And if you know me, you know that one of the ways to my heart is by coffee. Straight up, just bring me a cup of coffee with a heavy dose of creamer and I'll love you forever. Now, Jeff never brought me coffee when we were first dating because of the long distance. The few times we were actually together, he just didn't know that fact about me because, again, long distance. You just don't know those day in and day out things about the other person because you're never around them. If I'm honest with you, I'll say that this did factor into my breaking up with Jeff the first time. I just didn't think he liked me that much. It's a long story, but man, was I wrong. Wrong about Jeff not liking me that much and wrong that true love was summed up in a coffee drink!

I know now true love is about so much more than bringing you your favorite drinks. It's actually more about faithfulness, kindness, forgiveness and grace. However, knowing the little ways that show your person you like them and know them is important too and for me, that's coffee. Jeff knows that about me now and will bring me special drinks from time to time. I still remember the second year of marriage, he came home one day with two Starbucks red cups, the first of the season! Talk about TRUE LOVE!

Today, get your man his favorite drink. Maybe it's coffee like me or maybe it's a soda, Kombucha or a special water. Bring it to him at work, school or have it waiting for him at home. He'll love the kind gesture.

JOURNAL BELOW:

WRITE WHAT YOU LEARNED TODAY, HOW IT WENT AND WHAT MEMORIES WERE MADE.

DAY THIRTY: GIFTS

I'm not gonna lie. I love getting gifts! Not just any gift but ones that are super thoughtful and so me. When I open a gift from someone and it's exactly what I like, my heart is completely melted because I feel *known* and loved. It doesn't have to be anything big or expensive (I mean, this girl does love her diamonds, but really...). It can be the smallest thing (and honestly sometimes that's even better) like chocolate in a mason jar because those two things are my love language.

One time I had mentioned to my mom how much I love flowers and so I decided every time I go grocery shopping, I'm just going to buy myself a little bouquet of flowers as a treat to myself. Even if it's just one sunflower, it brings me so much joy to see it every time I walk past it or catch a glimpse of it. Since mentioning my love for flowers to my mom, she has brought me flowers every other week. Now, of course, I didn't tell my mom so she would buy me flowers. But because she is the most thoughtful person in the world, she always thinks of me when she runs into Safeway and will buy me a bouquet because she knows how much they mean to me (I know, she's the best)!

As much as I love receiving gifts, I like giving them even more. I love thinking of a gift that would bless someone I love. The best is when I'm out and about and I see something that screams one of my friends or family members. I have to get it. Even if it's a "just because" gift.

Gifts don't have to cost much at all; it can be the simplest thing, as long as it says "I'm thinking of you." Go out today and get a little something for your man. Maybe it's his favorite candy bar, a pair of his favorite socks, a few guitar picks, a new book that he's been wanting or a couple of movie tickets. Anything that says, "You are loved and known."

JOURNAL BELOW:

WRITE WHAT YOU LEARNED TODAY, HOW IT WENT AND WHAT MEMORIES WERE MADE.

DAY THIRTY-ONE: THANK-FULNESS

It's really easy to complain and think of all the things you'd like to be different right? Unfortunately, this is really easy to do when it comes to your man. There have been times when I let my mind wander and go down rabbit trails of how I'd like Jeff to be different. Or rather, things I'd like for him to do differently. How he can change. Areas he needs to grow in. Things I dislike; areas I get frustrated or irritated by. Yuck! Even just writing this out, I feel trapped and down.

It's good to see areas someone can grow in, to pray for them and encourage them to be the best version of themselves that they can be. It's never good to get in a pit of ungratefulness and complaining. It's toxic and not only will it bring you down, it will bring down the relationship.

Cultivating a heart of thankfulness is so vital in life, as well as in a relationship. Thinking of how thankful you are for your man and listing out ways that you're thankful for him is so important.

Todays task isn't so much for him but for you. Fostering a thankful heart for him will naturally overflow into your relationship and will affect how you see him. This will impact him because you'll become more joy-filled, grateful and kind, instead of complaining, nagging or harboring bitterness. Today list out ways that you are thankful for him. It can be the littlest thing to the biggest thing. Have fun seeing all the ways he is a blessing in your life!

JOURNAL BELOW:

WRITE WHAT YOU LEARNED TODAY, HOW IT WENT AND WHAT MEMORIES WERE MADE.

DAY THIRTY-TWO: YOUR TURN

You didn't think there was going to be a day 32 did ya? We thought we'd add one more day, to turn it over to you. Think of any idea, any gesture, or any kind thing you can do for your significant other today. Be creative. Be loving. And most of all show them how much you care. Also, we'd love to hear what you picked for day 32! We might even end up including it in future versions or volumes of this book. You can upload your idea at ***upload.31creativeways.com***. We can't wait to hear how creative you guys are and what y'all came up with!

JOURNAL BELOW:

WRITE WHAT YOU LEARNED TODAY, HOW IT WENT AND WHAT MEMORIES WERE MADE.

JOURNAL BELOW:

WRITE WHAT YOU LEARNED TODAY, HOW IT WENT AND WHAT MEMORIES WERE MADE.

A NOTE FROM US AFTER FINISHING THIS BOOK.

First off, you all rock! For reals. Complete rockstars. Why? Because you care about your relationship. You're investing in it. You believe in it. It matters to you.

We believe that a relationship is like a garden. For it to flourish it needs proper nourishment, constant care, awareness of the things trying to hurt it and sometimes is a little messy. This book is just a start to hopefully continuing or taking that leap of putting you and your significant other on the path to a vibrant and beautiful relationship.

So thank you for doing this journey with us. Thank you for reading this book. And thank you for just being you. We'd love to hear from you and how the challenge went by sharing something online with the hashtag #31creativeways. We are constantly on that hashtag to see all the awesome stuff you guys are doing, ways you tweaked one of our challenges to make it better and to see all the fun you're having!

WE DARE YOU TO TAKE OUR NEXT CHALLENGE.

Congrats on finishing 31 days!

We have included a preview from Love That Lasts (chapter 1 and chapter 6) which is a book we wrote to go along with the guidebooks. We hope our story encourages you!

lovethatlasts.co/newchallenge

LOVE THAT LASTS PREVIEW

CHAPTER 1

WHERE IS THE LOVE?

Jeff Bethke

I lost my virginity when I was sixteen.

In the back of a car.

In a church parking lot.

To someone who wasn't my girlfriend.

I know that's pretty forward, seeing as how we just met and all. But honestly, I don't say that to shock you. In fact, my intention is quite the opposite. According to stats, *that's normal*.

Oh, and did I mention that Alyssa didn't even hold someone's hand until we started dating in our twenties? To say our marriage was a collision of two very different stories would be an understatement. But that's Alyssa's story, and I'll let her tell that in the subsequent chapters.

When I think back to that time in my life, I shudder. I was plagued with debilitating insecurity, trying so hard to fit the mold projected as necessary to be popular. Isn't it interesting how much we sacrifice simply in hopes that others will like us and think we are cool?

I was searching—and searching desperately. I wanted to be liked, I wanted to be accepted. I wanted to be *known*. But from the outside I looked like a model kid. I was on the high school baseball team that played in two state championships in a row. My teachers usually told my mom that I was very bright but that I could probably apply myself a little more. I was the guy who seemed to have it all together. I spent an exhausting amount of energy on editing and protecting my image and caring about what others thought of me. And when you spend all your time on that, you have no time for anything else—yourself, your passions, your joy, following Jesus, and so on.

Filtering your life, or having others believe a lie about you (or at least a half-truth), is a full-time job.

I now see more clearly just how dark a time that was for me. If you were able to ask sixteen-year-old Jeff if he thought it was a dark time, I’m sure he’d say no. But that’s because I had nothing to compare it to. I thought being paralyzed by shame and guilt, not knowing what I was created for, and living for others’ approval was normal. That thinking culminated in a poor view of love, sexuality, and women that resulted in a string of terrible and unhealthy relationships and making bad decisions for years. And I’m still walking through the ramifications of that today.

High school was ground zero in many ways. The place where I began to make decisions that crashed in on me later.

We may not realize it, but many of us are playing a game of emotional and spiritual Jenga when it comes to romance, sexuality, and love. We make a lot of decisions that feel good in the moment, that seem like good ideas at the time, before we even consider their consequences. And just like in Jenga, every poor decision we make is another piece we remove from the tower, weakening our wholeness and humanness.

Most likely, it will all come crashing down. After a terrible breakup. An unhealthy relationship. Heartache. Fierce anger and bitterness.

It’s only *then* we realize it was the little decisions along the way that brought us to that point. The reason the breakup hurt so bad in college was because we set up unhealthy relationship patterns when we were fifteen. The reason our marriage starts to lose its foundation is that in our dating relationships in college we moved on to the next person as soon as the butterflies went away. The reason we almost cracked under the weight of shame after having sex with our boyfriend or girlfriend is because we spent years placing our identity not in Jesus but in purity rings and "true love waits" bracelets. Filtering your life, or having others believe a lie about you (or at least a half-truth), is a full-time job.

When we were actually making those decisions, nothing fell on our heads in those moments, so we thought we were in the clear. When we pulled a piece out of the tower, everything still held together.

When we said "just this once" and clicked on that link to watch porn. When we went to that party and made out with that person we never saw again. When we fantasized about that girl or made up a whole scenario or life with that guy who wasn't ours to think about in the first place.

When we stayed in the relationship even when all our friends and family said not to.

When we led that guy or girl on because we wanted to have control or feel wanted, even though we didn't really like them enough to date them.

So we kept going. We kept doing it.

Until one day, one particular decision became that final piece of Jenga—right when it was removed, it all fell apart. A pile at our feet.

I got married in my early twenties and quickly realized how those decisions and views and thoughts from ages ago were staring me in the face. I was fighting an uphill battle, one that was on a ninety-degree cliff.

I don’t think I’m alone in that feeling.

In fact, I’m a decade removed from that season in my life, and sometimes it feels like yesterday. There are images. Hundreds of images. Dozens of memories. Burned into the front of my brain.

And in some ways, I’m still haunted by those pictures and memories and thoughts. Sometimes following Jesus is gritty—blood, sweat, and tears type of stuff. There are moments when an uninvited, shameful memory jumps right in front of my concentration, and it takes everything in me—usually me lying on the floor, gritting my teeth, hands on my head—to remind myself of truth and ask: *What does God say about me in this moment? What does He say about Himself right now?*

That sixteen-year-old Jeff is dead. He was left in the grave, was nailed to the same cross Jesus was, the minute I said yes to following Him. I’m a new creation. Shame has been defeated. Jesus looks at me with searing, white-hot, ferocious love. I’m His.

This is the battleground of a healthy relationship: the mind. It starts there. Our thoughts can define us, and right views of God are the most important things about us because they create the entire trajectory of our lives.

Alyssa and I have battled with thoughts that harm our relationship. The way we see it, both of us came into our marriage sick in some way. A disease of sorts had been coursing through our systems for most of our lives, but sometimes it takes a marriage to start seeing the symptoms.

It reminds me of a party we had before we moved from Washington to Maui. We didn't know it at the time, but someone was definitely carrying a crazy intense virus. Within three days of the party, eleven of the fourteen people came down with a stomach bug that involved being wrapped around a toilet for two days straight, not knowing what end it was going to come out of next (and if you've been there, you know that might be one of the worst predicaments you can ever face in life).

When I was at the party, I didn't *feel* sick. I didn't *feel* like I caught anything. I didn't feel infected. In fact, I felt just the opposite. Happy, cheery, hanging out with friends and family. It wasn't until many days later that I actually *was* sick. Yet, I had *caught the virus* at the party days earlier.

In many ways, that's us with love.

We are lovesick and love diseased. Our views of romance, sexuality, dating, and marriage are killing us. We've been infected for years and haven't even realized it. It almost killed me in high school and stayed with me in college, like shrapnel in my soul that I'm still plucking out and finding healing for. Nothing has caused me more pain, grief, and hurt than previous relationships and my pursuit of love.

Isn't that true for most of us? We get to our midtwenties or midthirties and feel like we should be *beginning* our adult lives, yet it feels more like the end. We are tired. We are hurt. We are exhausted. And we don't want to do it anymore. We are left to pick up the pieces of our adolescence, and we now look back with enough perspective to realize just how detrimental our decisions have been.

How did we get here? Why are so many of us entering adult life, our marriages, jobs, and new families hanging on by a thread rather than starting our journey with vibrancy and life and fullness?

Maybe it has something to do with our bad definition of love.

Clearly something isn't working. Clearly we've got some wires crossed.

Our culture at large is hurt. Sick. Unhealthy. Bruised. Broken.

And a question that haunts me is, if we are *all* sick, do we realize how sick we truly are?

Loneliness has been declared an epidemic.

Porn has gotten so out of control, it's been labeled a “public health crisis” and “public hazard,” as Pamela Anderson, one of the most famous porn stars in history, put it.

The use of antidepressants has more than doubled since 1998.

“Friends with benefits” and “no strings attached” seem to be the normative view of most relationships—and of Hollywood movie titles.

Marriage is becoming so trivial, or is failing at such a high rate, that some lawmakers have considered things like a “two-year marriage license” instead of a lifetime commitment.

And selfish, casual, hookup sex has reached its logical conclusion in many ways. It has been so detached from an actual relationship that some people now buy lifelike robots that they can customize and have sex with. *I mean, if sex is simply about pleasuring yourself and getting what you want out of it, then why not get a robot instead of another human? They are much easier, and always “in the mood” as long as they’re plugged in.*

In a strange irony, one of the biggest pornography sites in the world, a place that is probably the farthest from real love, since you are literally having sex with yourself while staring at a computer screen, seems to be full of people in search of that very thing, as the most frequently used word in its comments section is *love*. Loneliness. Trivial marriages. Sex robots. Porn.

In a world where you can get anything you want at any time (as long as you have Amazon Prime or Postmates), love seems to be the proverbial carrot on a stick. Yet Scripture says that “God is love.”

And a famous quote says, “Every man who knocks on the door of a brothel is looking for God.”

But the good news is that the reverse is also true. God is knocking on the door of every brothel, looking for man. We all have our different brothels—places we go in search of connection, intimacy, and love. We need to be in a relationship because we are addicted to approval and that feeling of emotional and relational intimacy. For some, it’s the need to be recognized, liked, affirmed, and admired.

Or we scratch our heads, wondering why we so easily fall in and out of love with people we are dating, not realizing we are addicted to an ideal of a person who doesn’t exist, and our ideal not only crushes them but also doesn’t satisfy us. Then we move on, hoping to find it with the next person, creating a vicious cycle. We become human bodies full of wounds, hurts, emotions, and scars, carrying around so much baggage that we aren’t sure how much farther we can go. But what if it wasn’t actually love that got us to that place? What if it was the misunderstanding of love that did?

When I was sixteen and fresh out of driver’s ed, I had my first flat tire. I say “first,” because, well, let’s just say my first couple of years behind the wheel didn’t go so well. (If we ever have coffee, remind me to tell you about that one time I totaled my first car after only owning it for two weeks because I thought it would be a good idea to hydroplane purposely in big puddles for fun—with the car my dad had spent months building and repairing before giving it to me.)

I remember driving and feeling like something was a little off in the car’s movement. I was a few miles from home, driving on a side street after hanging out with some friends. (I can’t remember exactly what I was listening to but knowing the year, it was probably “Yeah” by Usher or “Boulevard of Broken Dreams” by Green Day. I may have an eclectic taste in music.) But it felt like the gas wasn’t working or that the emergency brake was on or the gas pedal needed to be pressed a little harder than usual to stay at a normal speed. It felt like I was towing or dragging something.

Since this was my first flat tire, I didn’t know what it was. I thought a flat tire would be more obvious. You know, like in the movies, where a tire explodes and the car spins out of control. At least in my case, driving felt off and weird, but I could still accelerate, turn, and stop.

But little did I know that every second I drove with a flat tire, the worse it was for my whole car—the rims, the engine, the alignment, and more. But I kept driving. And my car kept getting worse and worse and worse.

For a lot of us, the way we see love, dating, sexuality, marriage, and romance is like a flat tire. There’s a little something off at first. We know it and we feel it. Sure, we can still get from point A to point B on a flat tire. Sure, it does the job. Sure, sex before marriage doesn’t feel wrong. Sure, living together while you’re dating helps you learn more about each other. But there are moments when it feels “off.” There are moments when it feels more damaging than it should. But we don’t know any better, so we keep driving. And it gets worse. And worse. And worse.

We were created for more.

We were never meant to drive on a flat tire. We were never meant to have sex with someone who wasn’t our husband or wife. We were never meant to be addicted to porn. We were never meant to be so wrapped up in a relationship that makes us feel as if we are losing our god when we break up with that boyfriend or girlfriend. When we finally pull over, years later, to look under the hood, many of us realize—for the first time—just how damaging the flat tire was.

The years compounded have made us view love as something we can take instead of what we can receive.

As something we feel instead of something to commit to.

The reason love, romance, and sexuality feels so right, even when it’s wrong, is because we were created for it. Even the distortions hold an element of truth; that’s what a distortion is—an alteration of the original. But there’s more. So much more. God doesn’t want to take away our joy; He wants to give us more of it. He doesn’t want to take away our sexual desire; He wants to give us the context in which it works the best. God doesn’t want us to hate romance; He wants to introduce us to the greatest love story of all time.

In order to realize where we went so wrong, we first need to see where it was all so right. Where this intoxicating intimacy and love comes from in the first place.

As author Christopher West says, “Love, by its nature, desires to expand its own communion.” God didn’t need us. He was perfectly complete in and of Himself. But love creates. Love overflows. Love is abundance. Love is life. God made it so, simply out of the goodness of who He is, that He would create image bearers to share in that beautiful exchange of love. A beautiful picture of otherness becoming oneness. That’s what marriage vows mean. That’s what sex is in body. And that’s what covenant is in promise.

Love creates. Love overflows. Love is abundance. Love is life.

We can□t miss the truth found in that beautiful divine and mysterious and glorious moment. That when He created us and all the uniqueness of male and female bodies, He was choosing to communicate something about Himself. One of the first commands in all Scripture is to have sex. Well, God□s exact words are "be fruitful and multiply" (Genesis 1_28), but you get the idea. Because even before sin entered the world, male and female were incomplete and were built with a longing, a holy longing for the otherness to become oneness. That□s the story we were created to tell.

As the poet Wendell Berry put it, "The sexuality of community life is centered on marriage, which joins two living souls as closely as, in this world, they can be joined. This joining of two who know, love, and trust one another brings them in the same breath in the freedom of sexual consent and into the fullest earthly realization of the image of God. From their joining, other living souls come into being, and with them great responsibilities that are unending, fearful, and joyful." It□s striking to me how often sexuality and the Christian religion face off as enemies in various cultures, when in reality, nothing or no one has a more dynamic, powerful, beautiful, weighty, and incredible view of sexuality than the follower of Jesus does. That very moment when husband and wife come together in perfect love—not only in Spirit and in soul, but also in their bodies—is one of the clearest pictures we have of God. It□s telling a story.

And God created our bodies so that we could partake in that story. Sexuality. Male. And female. That we might be "other" but come together as one. That there might be a communion of persons and an exchange of love. That when brought together, they produce a "third" image.

In the first couple of words of Scripture (Genesis 1_1), an assumption is made: "In the beginning, God created the heavens and the earth," which implies that before those things were created, God still was, and is, and is to come. He was there before anything. And immediately we get a hint as well at the divine mystery that is the Trinity. He says, "Let us make man in our image" (Genesis 1_26), implying a plurality, yet at the same time we see the obvious singularity of this Creator. It takes a while for the scriptures to fully unpack this beautiful truth, but as they do so we can read backward and see from that very moment God is and always has been an endless cycle and circle of love. The perfect picture of three persons yet oneness—the Father, the Son, and the very Spirit of God—eternally surrendering and submitting and exalting one another. So when God says let Us make man in Our image in Genesis 1, that means humans are born out of the overflow of God's very own image. We are born out of that. And whatever we are created *out of*, also is what we were created *for*.

At its core, sexuality is an expression of the mystery of the Trinity. An opportunity to tell the greatest story ever told: that somehow there are more than one, yet somehow there is one.

Our bodies are telling this story.

This is why children and marriage are meant to happen together. Marriage is two becoming one; then children are born out of the overflow of love and oneness. They are image bearers. They are mini images that the love created.

Of course, things don't always happen how they should. We must face the fact that we are born into a curse-stricken world.

Infertility. Broken marriages. Even the deaths of children. Yet there is so much grace and so much healing in Jesus for all of us. In fact, I think the reason infertility is so painful is that our souls echo, *This isn't how it should be*. And as Scripture shows us, *how it should be* can also teach us about how it is.

Our love yearns for an outlet. For an overflow. In Scripture it's clear that Jesus is in the business of redemption, of new creation, and of telling His story. That happens every day in two-parent homes, one-parent homes, infertility homes, adoption homes, miscarriage homes, and so on. Our love yearns for an outlet. For an overflow. In Scripture it's clear that Jesus is in the business of redemption, of new creation, and of telling His story. That happens every day in two-parent homes, one-parent homes, infertility homes, adoption homes, miscarriage homes, and so on.

For some, that overflow of love carries over into work. Notice how God Himself was eternal love first, and then He created. The endless love of God bubbled up into earth and heaven and skies and moon and sun and animals and ultimately us. Creation was born out of love.

Yet our culture also idolizes work. Too many people exhaust themselves and sacrifice their families and marriages in the process. But godly work flows from the covenant of love. Not the other way around. In Scripture, marriage is an overflow of love. It is no coincidence that the Bible begins and ends with a marriage.

Adam and Eve in Genesis.

Jesus and His church in Revelation.

If you could summarize the Bible succinctly, it would be about God creating, looking for, pursuing, and restoring a bride. A people for Himself. To be called into that oneness.

It□s why all the love stuff—those butterflies, dating, romance, marriage, intimacy, sex, and that deep connection you feel when you□re both vulnerable and fully loved at the same time—is not about us. In the end, we are just reflections.

A couple of years ago, I had the opportunity to travel to Morocco and be on the set during a week of shooting for the production of a huge TV show that would air during prime time on NBC later that year. To say it was as big as it gets is an understatement. They built lifelike sets in the middle of the desert. I remember the distinct feeling of awe and amazement I experienced all week. It felt surreal not only to be on a set larger than life, but also to peek behind the curtain and see just how they make movie and TV magic. It was incredible.

My friend, who traveled with me, and I got to hang out in a tent where we wore headphones connected to all the other audio sets (the director, the actors, and so on). One of my favorite things was listening to the director do his job. When I watch shows on TV, I only see the final product, but being there on set, I got to look behind the scenes to the why. I got to see why the director had those characters stand there and say their lines with a particular intonation, and why he chose that camera angle—all to further the story.

I remember thinking, *That's exactly what marriage is like*. It□s a peek behind the curtain.

It's the Creator of the universe coming down to us at the wedding ceremony and whispering, "Hey, you want to know what I'm like? You want to know how I love? You want to know how I relate to you as humans? Here ya go. Here's your picture."

And that's why ultimately love in us is only a reflection of the true thing. Like those actors on the set, or me as a kid when I put on my Superman outfit, we are pointing to a reality, but we are not the reality itself. In those moments it's real, but it's not the ultimate reality, which is why when we are fully joined in union with God at the end of time, there will be no marriages. You don't need the shadow when the real thing is in front of you.

And that's God with us. His love is the reality. His ferocious pursuit of us is the real thing. Our job is to reflect His love back to Him. And in marriage and romance and sexuality, we get to learn what that means. We get to learn what it means to love unconditionally. What it means to pursue no matter what. What it means to forgive endlessly. What it means to serve without condition.

I distinctly remember a little whisper in my soul when I was sixteen years old in the back of that car in the church parking lot. I knew what we were doing wasn't it. That wasn't what I was created for. I was telling a lie. With my body. And with my life. But it took me years to fully realize that and pick up the pieces.

In that particular season of my life, I came to recognize, as Ronald Rohreiser put it, that sex could not "deliver the goods." He continues by explaining how sex alleviates our loneliness too little. Especially our moral loneliness. Sex that isn't sublime doesn't bring us a soul mate.

What it brings is a fix. A hit. A drug. That helps us through a lonely night or lonely season. But deep down we know it cannot give us what we need. Sex cannot be sublime without first living a real chastity. The person who sleeps with someone he or she hardly knows, has no real commitment to, and has never lived a chaste tension with, will not have a sublime or profound experience. Short-circuiting chastity is like trying to write a masterpiece overnight. Good luck. But it isn’t going to happen. Great love, like great art, takes great effort, sustained commitment, and lots of time.

While cheap sex might not be what you are exchanging for true love, many of us often put something else in its place.
A feeling.
A fairy tale.
A substance.
Disillusionment.
Serial relationships.
But those aren’t love. And, like Rohreiser says, great love takes effort and commitment and lots of time—because it’s in those things that the depth and beauty and mystery of a true love will show itself superior to the false realities, the lesser reflections we cheapen it with.

TAKEAWAY

Before God’s vision for healthy relationships can fully develop, we have to detox from poor, harmful, and parodied versions of love, sex, marriage, and dating.

Alyssa Bethke

I had my first “real boyfriend” at age twenty-two. I’d spent so much time waiting and longing to be married. When I was in college, I’d prayed for my future husband. I asked the Lord to make our relationship a “were it not for God” one. You know, the kind that is so evidently created by God, the couple who is so good together that only God could’ve written their love story because it was too good to be true, too beautiful a story to have just happened. I wanted a relationship that I could tell others was “all God.” I wanted to be able to point to God’s faithfulness and share how He answered all those prayers for all those years and . Well, He did just that.

In the spring of 2009, I graduated from a college in Los Angeles and looked forward to a two-year internship I had lined up at a church on Maui. After I said goodbye to my roommates and friends in LA in August, I headed back home to Seattle for two weeks. I was so excited to go home for a bit after months of hardship and extreme loneliness. I was also eager to hop on a plane at the end of my visit to see what was waiting for me out there in the Pacific.

While home, I planned to attend the wedding of my friend Stacey. Her younger brother and sister, Jake and Shannon, were two of my closest friends. We’d grown up together in church and had a really close-knit youth group. We did everything together back then, and many of us were home for the wedding. I’m still close to those friends today.

A few days before the wedding, I joined my friends at the church to help set up for the reception. We stopped to buy lunch, and as we sat on the old gymnasium floor to eat burgers and fries, my friend Shannon declared, in front of our big circle of friends, “Lyss, I know someone who is smitten with you!” (Shannon grew up on old movies, has a love for older eras, and uses words like *smitten*.)

I blushed. And also was completely confused because I hadn’t been home very often during the last couple of years. Who in the world would have a crush on me? Who even knew me?

All the girls asked, *“Who?”*

“Bethke!”

At first, I had no idea who she was talking about. Bethke? Who is Bethke? Then I remembered he was Shannon’s brother’s best friend. He had requested to be my friend on Facebook months before and sent me a couple of messages, but I hadn’t thought much of it since I didn’t actually know him. I remembered meeting him at our high school prom. He had been the guy onstage, wearing sunglasses and getting everyone pumped up to dance. He had been the center of attention. The life of the party.

All the girls started to giggle and talk about this Bethke guy. I’ll admit, I was totally flattered and a bit excited. I remembered his photo. He was cute. And it had been so long since someone had actually liked me. But mostly I played it cool. I was leaving in a week for an island two thousand miles away in the middle of the Pacific Ocean. If anything, I had my heart set on meeting a surfer boy and falling in love under the Maui moon.

Starting a relationship with a boy I barely knew, who was younger than me, and—as I came to find out—was leaving for college in Oregon in a week, was totally out of the question. I mean, we went to the same high school and never even hung out. Why would anything spark between us now?

I couldn’t stop wondering about Jeff Bethke though. Confession: I totally stalked his Facebook profile. Isn’t that what it’s for? There were so many pictures of him and Jake hanging out. I gathered that he liked camping and dogs and was a leader on the baseball field. There was even a video of him sharing the gospel with eightyear-olds at a summer youth sports camp. *Okay, God, I’ll be open. If you want to strike up an interaction, that’d be nice.* Not to mention he was super attractive. On the day of the wedding, Shannon mentioned that Jeff was coming just to meet me. He hadn’t been invited, but her mom said he could come if he helped clean up afterward. I wore my best dress and curled my hair. Then I waited and waited and waited for him to come up and talk to me. The wedding ceremony came and went.

Finally, after the cake had been cut, Jeff walked over to my table, hugged me like we’d known each other for years, and started talking. I was taken aback by how familiar he seemed, how easy the conversation was, and how comfortable I felt with him. We talked as if we were best friends. Jeff shared how he had given his life to Jesus a couple of years back in college and how he’d been growing as a Christian ever since. I don’t remember much more about the conversation, but I remember thinking, *There’s something different about this guy.* I wanted to know more. He was so open, honest, and deep right away, and I knew he was the real deal in terms of his walk with Jesus.

That week, we ended up hanging out quite a few times with a bunch of our friends. At church. Feasting on late-night milkshakes and burgers. And at one last bonfire before we said goodbye to summer.

Jake had texted, asking if I wanted to come over for the bonfire. It was kind of a going-away party for Jeff before he left for college the next morning, but it was also my last night before I flew out to Maui. I told him I'd be over after dinner with my parents.

Little did I know that Jake and Jeff had been conspiring all week, planning different times for Jeff and me to see each other.

We all stood or sat around the bonfire, talking and laughing and roasting marshmallows. At one point, Jeff and I found ourselves sitting beside the campfire alone (sneaky friends!), and it was then that Jeff opened up more about his past. I liked how nothing was hidden with him. While he was sharing, his marshmallows caught on fire. He tried to blow out the flames, but as he did, they dropped in his lap—crotch on fire! He quickly patted his shorts down but then had gooey marshmallows all over. He was a total mess.

While Jeff left to clean up, I hung out with friends who had returned to the bonfire. When he came back, he wore a new pair of shorts and smelled of heavy cologne. *This guy is totally into me*, I thought. And I was totally interested in him.

I stayed as long as I could, knowing that if I stayed up too late when I had an early flight the next morning, I'd regret it. I just wanted Jeff to give some indication that we'd stay in touch. He still hadn't even asked for my phone number.

Finally, I stood up and told everyone I had to go.

Jeff jumped up and blurted out, “Um, so do you have a phone?”

I tried not to giggle. *Dude, it’s the twenty-first century.*

“Yeah,” I said coyly.

Clearing his throat, Jeff asked, “Um, can I get your number then?”

I gave him my number, hugged him, and left. I didn’t know what would happen, but at least there was hope as we went our separate ways.

During the next couple of months, Jeff called me and we’d end up on the phone for hours. He was so easy to talk to. There was never a lull in the conversation, and what we did talk about was encouraging and soul-filling. Jeff was smart and made me think about things differently.

Then suddenly, that October, I didn’t hear from him. Not once. No phone calls. No text messages. No Facebook. I totally thought he was over me. I figured it was just too hard being that far apart. I still thought about him a lot but honestly just didn’t see how it’d work out anyway, so I gave up.

Then suddenly, that October, I didn’t hear from him. Not once. No phone calls. No text messages. No Facebook. I totally thought he was over me. I figured it was just too hard being that far apart. I still thought about him a lot but honestly just didn’t see how it’d work out anyway, so I gave up.

Then, out of the blue, that November, he called me and talked to me as if nothing were amiss. (*Hello . . . I haven't heard from you in a month!*) After a few minutes, he jumped into a spiel about how he had been listening to a sermon and the pastor was saying that when you find a girl who loves Jesus, don't let her go. Go after her. He told me he realized that he didn't want to let me go and asked if I'd be his girlfriend. He wanted to see where things could go with us and intentionally wanted to get to know me better to see if maybe marriage was in our future. It all felt so right. I had never met anyone like Jeff before, and even though I had no idea how it would work out, I really wanted to get to know him better too. So I agreed. And so began our relationship.

We talked on the phone regularly and texted and e-mailed each other. (Yes, email. It was a thing back then.) We had to be creative with how we pursued each other, being two thousand miles away. We would send each other cards and gifts. I remember making him a Thanksgiving card, a turkey made out of my thumbprint, and sending him a candy gram for Valentine's Day. I made him homemade puppy chow (Chex mix covered in peanut butter, chocolate, and powdered sugar. I mean, if that doesn't win a guy's heart, I don't know what will! Well, maybe a steak.) and sent it in a box, and I still remember him calling to thank me as he shoveled it into his mouth.

When I went home for Christmas that year, we finally got to spend time together in face-to-face. It was a little awkward at first because we hadn't been together in person much more than a few days, and now all of a sudden we were together as a couple. But we spent almost every day together. We laughed and talked about everything and anything. The more I hung out with him, the more I liked him. In fact, by the end of the two weeks, I was totally in love. Head in the clouds and over so clumsy all the time because, honestly,

I was always thinking of Jeff. My mom noticed it too. She just laughed at how crazy I was about this guy.Throughout the rest of that school year, I saw Jeff every couple of weeks. I flew to visit him at college for a weekend, and when his baseball team came to Oahu for a tournament, I hopped islands with my friend Risa to see him. Then he came out in May to visit for two weeks. I was so excited, I couldn't contain myself! Finally, we were going to be with each other for a good chunk of time.

I had all these hopes and expectations for our time together. Though I still had to work for a church for one of the weeks Jeff was here, I figured he would come to the events with me or would hang out in the office during the day, and we would do fun things together before and after work. Ride bikes to a local breakfast spot, play tennis, read our Bibles at Starbucks (because, clearly, that's what a Christian couple does!). My parents were flying out for the other week and had rented a hotel room for all of us as a vacation.

Those two weeks with Jeff were like a roller coaster. Big highs and low lows. Well, in my heart anyway. On the surface, we were great. We played in the pool, walked the beach, gallivanted around the island. But the whole time, I felt like Jeff was holding back. Honestly, I had begun to wonder if he even liked me anymore. I was afraid that I was totally in love with this guy, that I was ready to say yes if he popped the question, but he wasn't really feeling it in return. He wasn't very affectionate, and the one time I tried to bring up the *M* word, he quickly changed the conversation, as if he *was* terrified.

The week that I had to work, he didn't visit me at the church one time. I had to beg him to come to youth group with me. Looking back, I think I had these dreams of us being a team and me being on mission with my boyfriend, but it didn't seem like Jeff and me being on mission with my boyfriend, but it didn't seem like Jeff wanted to join me. I was so torn. I loved him. He gave me butterflies all the way to my toes, and I'd never met a guy who loved Jesus the way he did. But after I dropped him off at the airport, I knew we needed to break up.

It hit me the night I was flying out with some of my youth group to go on a twoweek mission trip. I had just gotten off the phone with my mom, telling her my doubts about Jeff, that he didn't seem to like me much. How would we even work? He was still in college, with one more year to go. I didn't want to leave Maui ever, and he wanted to stay in the Pacific Northwest forever. He certainly wasn't ready to commit to marriage, and I was ready to move forward.

I thought he'd want to be more a part of my life by helping out with the high schoolers at the church and seeing what I did day to day, but instead he kept his distance. As the plane took off that night, big tears dropped onto my cheeks. I knew I had to break up with him. Later that night, I put my face into my pillow and cried until I fell asleep, and I did that every night for most of that mission trip. When I got home, there was a package waiting on the front porch with my name on it from Jeff. My heart sank a little. I brought it inside, plopped it on my bed, and opened it. There was a long handwritten note saying how much he liked me, what a great time he'd had while in Maui, and how much he missed me. Then, below the note was his favorite baseball sweatshirt. I pulled it out of the box and held it up to my nose. Sean Jean. Jeff had sprayed it with his cologne. He knew how much I loved his scent and would always spray his letters with his cologne. The only thing better was a sweatshirt so that when I wore it, it smelled just like him.

Sigh.

This certainly didn’t make breaking up with him any easier. He had no idea what was coming.

I waited as long as I could, but finally called the next day. He knew something was up. Why else would I have waited to call him?

We talked and caught up for a couple of minutes, and then I laid it on him.

“Jeff, I have to break up with you.”

“What, why?”

“I don’t know why, really. I just know I need to call things off.”

“But I don’t understand. *Why?*”

I tried to explain myself, but I couldn’t. I had doubts, but I couldn’t quite wrap my mind around them. I loved him, and yet it seemed wrong. The worst part, though, was that I couldn’t share any of my true thoughts or reasons with Jeff, because I didn’t know how to handle conflict. How could I possibly tell him something that would hurt him? How could I tell him how I really felt? About doubts I was having? And besides, even if I did, I already had decided in my heart of hearts what to do. There was no turning back now. The worst part of all was that after two weeks of crying, I had no emotions left. I was as stoic as a statue. No emotions. No tears.

Nothing.

Jeff cried. It□s still the only time I□ve ever heard him cry. I thought, *Maybe this guy really does like me after all.*

"Well, could we just take a break? Can we see how things go?"

"No. We□re done. Forever."

I was brutal.

Months passed, and they were the hardest few months of my life. I thought that since I was the one to break up, I should be strong and ready to move on. But in reality, I was just as broken. Morning after morning I would sit on my cushy, wornout, gray couch, with my coffee in one hand and Bible and journal in my lap, as big teardrops decorated the pages.

Why, God? Why couldn't he have been the one? Why did I have to fall so hard for him? Why did I break up with him? Why wasn't it right?

That summer I fought the fears that had been building my whole life. *What if I never get married? What if I'm alone forever?*

TAKEAWAY

Sometimes relationships bring up deep fears and questions. God never deserts us. He wants us to share those fears and questions with Him.

Get the whole Love That Lasts Experience at

lovethatlasts.co/newchallenge

OTHER RE- SOURCES

For those who maybe are getting this as a gift or don't know much about us, below are just a few other things we have created and done over the past few years. We hope they encourage you!

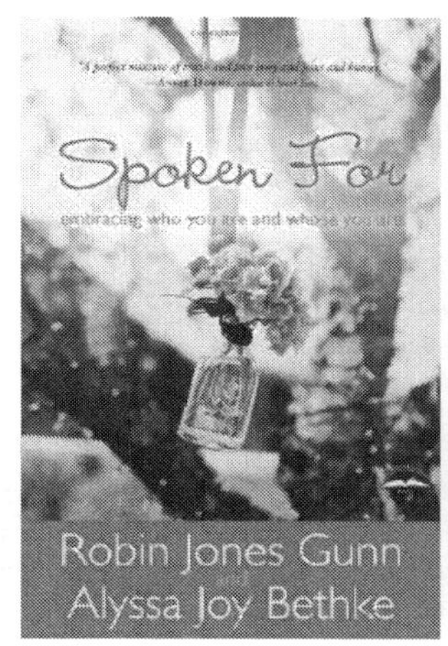

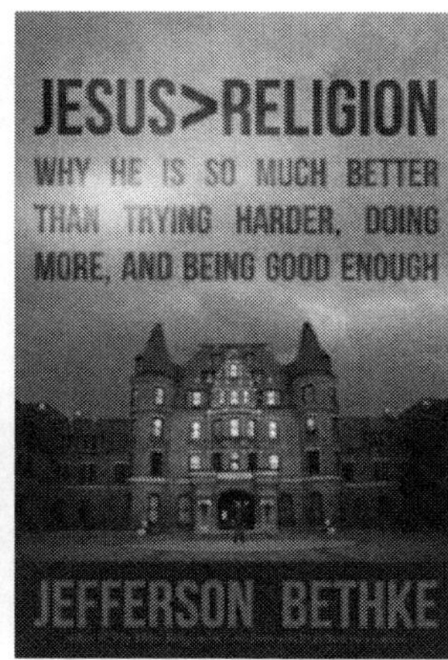

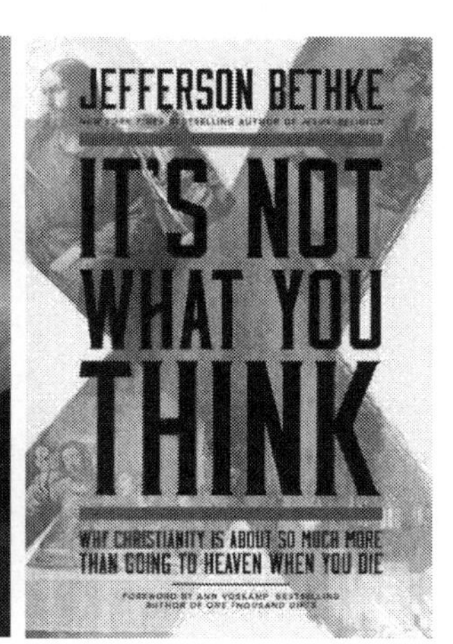

Find at
JEFFANDALYSSA.COM

Find at
BETHKEWORKSHOPS.COM

WHERE TO FIND US ONLINE.

We love when folks give us a shout on social media,
so feel free to stop by and say hey!
Would love to e-meet you.

PODCAST

lovethatlasts.co/podcast

INSTAGRAM

@jeffersonbethke
@alyssajoybethke

TWITTER

@jeffersonbethke
@alyssajoybethke

FACEBOOK

fb.com/jeffersonbethkepage
fb.com/alyssajoybethke

SNAPCHAT

jeffersonbethke

WEBSITES

jeffandalyssa.com
bethkeworkshops.com
31creativeways.com
lovethatlasts.co

We are always looking for great things to help marriages and relationships. We've found a few we absolutely love and hope you guys will too!

DATEBOX:

We LOVE this. It's a subscription service that sends you a fully curated Datebox every month to your doorstep. For example, during the Christmas season in December we got a box that included a gingerbread making kit, two custom mugs, hot cocoa mix, a Christmas playlist and bunch more goodies.

We wanted to hook you guys up to check it out. Use "LOVETHATLASTS" it gives you your first FREE box.

Made in the USA
Middletown, DE
18 February 2020